JACK

THE COMEBACK KID

EVA COLE

JACK THE COMEBACK KID

ISBN: 979-8-234-20181-2

Dedicated to:

Peter Telemark, John Cole, Sr., Joyce Twistol-Rafferty, James Rafferty, Roxanne Twistol, My Worldwide Team: Josh in Kansas, Mark in California, Anriette from Armenia/California, Helen and Mengyi from China/California, Justin from Missouri/California. Todd from Korea/California, Kazuaki 和聡和聡 藤渡 (Kanji) in Japan.

Thank you to my current and longtime mentors:

- Louis D'Esposito, Co-President at Marvel Studios.
- Calvin Brown, Jr., Emmy Award Winning Executive Producer and Writer at Disney Animation.
- Mike Detillier, College/Pro Football Analyst, Co-Host of SportsTalk at WWL Radio in New Orleans and Host of Sports on the Bayou TV Show.

Special Thank You's

Kathy Jacobson at NFL Films. Kirk McGowan in Urbandale, Iowa. Jason Miller, President at Fins Up So Cal Fan Club. All members at Fins Up So Cal Fan Club. Marc Angelo, President at NorCal Dolfan Club. All members at NorCal Dolfan Club. All members, fan-friends and employees at Miami Dolphins. Fans of all NFL teams.

This book is for:

Preface

Jack the Comeback Kid isn't just a story about football. It's a poignant coming-of-age story filled with issues that speak to teens and young adults. This story inspires young readers in ways that are relevant to their lives. Many young people grapple with issues like:

* *Pressure from their parents*

* *Fears of failing*

* *Never feeling good enough*

* *A constant need for approval*

* *Discovering who they really are*

Jack's struggles will help young adults know that they're not alone in their battles. An Empowering Message About Self-Worth.

Jack the Comeback Kid

is perfectly suited for:

- ★ sports camps
- ★ summer camps
- ★ school reading programs
- ★ youth leadership groups
- ★ teen mentorship programs

LESSONS FROM THE FIELD

Important lessons young athletes can learn:

JACK'S GAME PLAN
HEALTHY HABITS FOR VICTORY
EXERCISE
HEALTHY EATING & LIVING
DEDICATION
SELF-DISCIPLINE

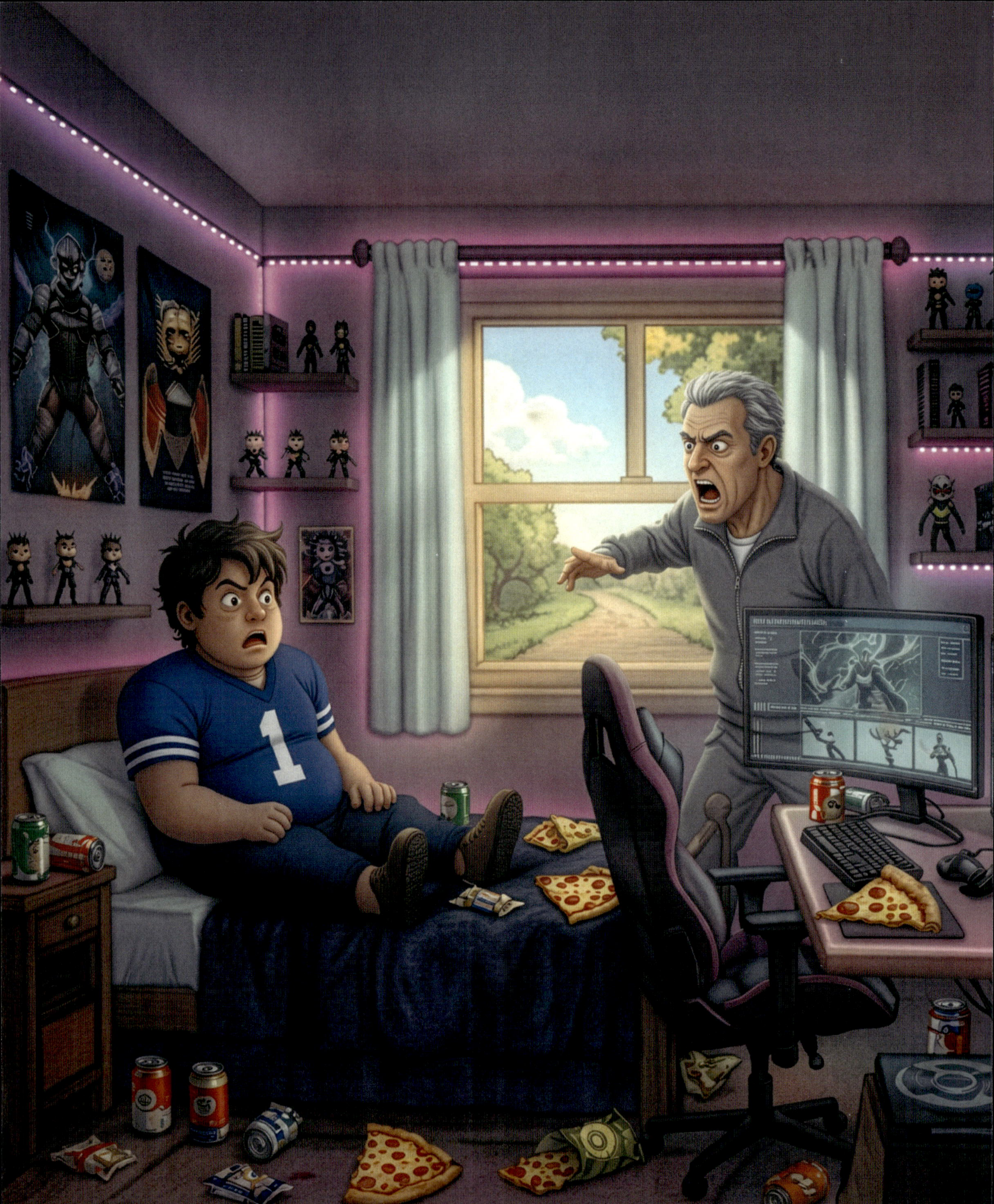
1

JACK

THE COMEBACK KID

"You'll always be a loser."

Even hours later, his dad's words still stung. In Jack's house in Urbandale, Iowa - it was just him and his dad, his mom having left long ago because of her husband's endless criticism.

Although he was only a teen, Jack understood his dad. A wannabe high school footballer who never made the cut but wanted his son to succeed where he had failed.

So, from the moment he could walk, Jack was pressured about football. Dad had high hopes that Jack would become a star footballer in high school. The only time he spent with Jack was when practicing throws and catches. If "ambition" were a sport, Dad's trophy case would be overflowing.

He even insisted that Jack call him "Coach Dad" – although "Couch Dad" would have been more fitting. He had spent so much time sitting there watching football that the cushion developed a permanent imprint of his behind.

The only problem was that Jack hated football.

He didn't want to play. He resented his father for pressuring him, to the point of making him wear a football jersey and helmet at home whenever he watched TV sports (mainly football).

But there was a way out. He could eat his way out. If he got too fat and flabby, there wasn't any chance he could make the cut. No chance meant no pressure.

PCIDLTS
FOOTHIL

So, he surrendered to pizza, candy bars, gooey cheeseburgers, fries, and especially potato chips when watching TV. It didn't take long for his plan to succeed.

When Dad wasn't throwing the ball with him (or was it "at him"?), Jack could be found in his game room in front of the TV. But not watching sports. Playing video games. With one hand on the controller and the other clutching pizza, chips, cola, or enough candy to induce a diabetic coma.

He'd show Dad!

Eventually, by the age of 15, he was big enough for football. But he was in no shape to play it.

Did that stop Coach Dad? Not hardly! When Junior Varsity tryouts for Farmdale High School's Blue Snakes came along, there also came an ultimatum: "You're going. Or else I'll put a padlock on the refrigerator!"

Jack's stomach groaned with alarm. But he knew he had no choice but to obey. He was confident he would fail spectacularly. On the other hand, he didn't look forward to being the school's laughingstock.

At the tryout, Jack stumbled onto the practice field, feeling he was about to make the biggest fool of himself. He made up his mind he wouldn't deliberately fail. He would try his best.

Coach McGowan tried to hide his skepticism. He was not unkind, but he had an obligation to build a winning team.

"Alright, son, let's see your talent."

It turned out Jack only had a talent for tripping, fumbling catches, and throwing passes into the bleachers.

That didn't go unnoticed by the other boys. Jack hadn't expected applause, but the last thing he wanted was jeers.

At the end, Coach McGowan tried to be kind.

“Son, you made a good try, but...”

"...not even close!" Dad snarled at him on the way home. That's when he told Jack he would always be a loser.

That night, the refrigerator was not locked. His Dad had given up on him.

But Jack made up his mind. He would not give up.

He remembered his one-time friend, Luke, who had been the Varsity quarterback a couple of years earlier. However, a brutal tackle had broken his leg and forced him to quit. That leg had never mended properly.

Jack had always admired him for the way he handled it. No bitterness, no guilt. Just grateful that he had the chance to play the sport he loved.

If anyone could help him get into shape, Luke was the one. It didn't take long to enlist his sympathy and his help.

It started slowly. More walking than sitting, water instead of cola, salads instead of burgers.

It wasn't easy. Whenever his stomach growled, he imagined persistent whispers from the potato chip bag in the cupboard:

"Jaaack, eat us. We're crispy...we're salty. Give in."

But he didn't, although other temptations came his way. Once, after a hard workout with Luke, he saw his dad munching a donut. Its unforgotten taste made his tongue tingle. But he firmly swatted that away.

"Not today, you sugary traitor."

Over time, he lost weight and gained muscle. And practiced with Luke. Throwing and catching passes until dusk. Running miles, lifting weights. And watching games – not for Dad but for himself.

Somewhere along the way, he started liking football – how each player became part of something bigger than himself, sharing a purpose and a meaning.

For the first time, the idea of playing football became Jack's own choice. Funny how that works – when it's your idea, it's way cooler. He now seriously thought about being a quarterback.

Finally, the Varsity tryouts came around and Jack was ready. When Coach McGowan saw him, he could hardly recognize him.

"You've been doing some training." He waved him onto the practice field. At the end of the tryout, the coach clapped him on the shoulder. "Jack, there's a place for you on our team."

Jack started to grin, but then Coach continued, "Not as quarterback, of course. We already have our guy. You'll play tight end."

Inwardly, Jack groaned. All those practice passes and catches with Luke! But he only straightened his shoulders and said, "Yes, sir. Thank you."

For even if he didn't get his dream assignment, he had still made the cut. He was going to play football!

Did that satisfy Dad? Maybe a little, but now more pressure was heaped on him to "Win! Win! Win!" as if that depended on Jack alone.

On game night, the stadium was alive with excitement. Mostly from what happened on the field, but sometimes from a fan dropping their cheesy nachos onto the head of someone sitting in front.

Soon, the Blue Snakes dominated the match.

Jack played tough, blocked tough, gave his all. Things went well for the Blue Snakes. But in the fourth quarter, the unthinkable happened.

After the snap, the quarterback couldn't find any free receivers. He panicked as the linebackers closed in. Then, he spotted his tight end not far from the goal line.

“Jaaack!”

The ball flew like a missile to Jack's waiting hands. The crowd gasped with anticipation as he sprinted for the goal line.

Ten yards away.

Now, five.

The line was just inches away...

Suddenly, he was tackled! Just inches from the end zone!

The crowd groaned. But only one voice rubbed it in.

"Loser!" his father yelled with disgust.

But the Blue Snakes won anyway. The quarterback was carried on his team's joyful shoulders as they paraded him to the locker room.

And where was Jack? Trailing silently after them, wishing he could crawl inside his locker. He didn't go to the after-game party with the others. He quietly slinked outside, afraid of his father's reaction.

But "Coach Dad" was nowhere in sight. He had already left. Jack felt even more humiliated and started walking home as streetlamps began to glow. Somewhere in the night sky behind them, the lights on the scoreboard winked off.

He had not gotten far when Luke came hobbling up behind him.

“Wait up, Jack!”

Jack was almost tempted to keep walking. He felt bad enough and didn’t need to hear his friend’s disappointment. But he couldn’t turn his back on Luke.

He waited until his friend caught up with him.

“Hey, man,” Luke said breathlessly, “you played a heck of a game.”

Jack looked at him like he was crazy. “Oh, right. All the way until getting tackled. Maybe Dad is right. I’m a loser, after all.”

Luke smiled and laid a hand on his shoulder. “I felt that way after I broke my leg. But I don’t anymore...

Jack shook himself from his self-pity and gave Luke his full attention.

“You know,” Luke continued, “a lot of people think football is only about winning and getting applause. But you can’t tell me you made your comeback – pushing yourself to the limit, sacrificing foods you love – just to get a handclap from your dad?”

After some thought, Jack replied, “No. I did it because I grew to love football – to be part of the team, part of the football community. It gave me a direction. I felt like I meant something.”

“You do mean something. Getting tackled didn’t change that. It doesn’t matter what anyone else thinks. You gave the sport your all - all your heart.”

And Jack understood at last

1

When you try at something with all your heart – whether you win or not – you can never be a loser.

That was Jack's comeback.

THE END

WINNING
DOESN'T DETERMINE
YOUR WORTH

Made in the USA
Coppell, TX
16 June 2026

81388665R00036